ENJOYING THE FRUIT OF THE SPIRIT WITH THE GIFTS OF THE SPIRIT

BY LEBOGANG MERRIAM SEOKETSA

DEDICATION

Praise the Lord

I would like to honor and praise God, my Lord and Savior Jesus and the Holy Spirit who is my Teacher, my Helper, my guider and my Advocate for helping me to write this book.

I would like to thank God and dedicate this book:

To my parents; my husband – Monty Seoketsa, my daughters – Dipolelo, Remoikantse and my brother – David and his daughter, Koketso.

To the mothers who always pray for me: Mrs. Joyce Molepo, Mrs. Anna Monama, Mrs. Dorcus Skosana.

To my Pastors and Lecturers of International Pentecostal Bible Institute: Pastor Pretorius, Pastor Mofomme and Pastor Phefadu.

To my Pastor, advisor and my well-wisher of The Fountain of Praise and Worship Church: Pastor MS Mogoane and his wife (Always there)

ACKNOWLDEGEMENT

Without the help of the Holy Spirit who was promised to us by our Lord Jesus Christ, nothing in life can be successful. This is the result of the contribution of many individuals who directly and indirectly share their gifts, talents and not forgetting wisdom of which our Lord said in James 1:5 "If any of you lacks wisdom, he should ask God, who gives generously to all without finding fault, and it will be given to him."

I wish to thank my husband, Monty, and our daughters Dipolelo and Remoikantse for their love, patience (fruit of the Spirit) and understanding for staying long hours on the computer, late nights and early mornings writing. This achievement is also yours.

ABOUT THE AUTHOR

Dr. Lebogang Merriam Seoketsa is married to Mr. Monty Seoketsa and they are blessed with two daughters. She earned her Doctor of Ministry from Team Impact Christian University and M-Tech in Public Management from Tshwane University of Technology. She is currently working as departmental administrator and she worked as part-time lecturer in the department of Public Management - Tshwane University of Technology. She worked with different committees in different projects. She taught about deliverance to different groups. She is the founder of the ministry "Your Burden is my Burden" (Galatians 6:2). The ministry is taking care of the needy families. "I am holding on to the Word of God to carry the Great Commission."

"I am holding on to the Word of God to carry the Great Commission."

The book Enjoying the fruit of the Spirit.....was written to make believers aware that we cannot seek the gifts without first acquiring the Fruit. We must have the fruit of the Spirit at work, and enjoy them if we want God to entrust us with the gifts of the Spirit. If we have word of wisdom, then we must have love. Word of knowledge will be received with joy. If we have the peace that passes all understanding then we will be ready for the gift of Faith. If we can learn to be Longsuffering in all, then we will be able to accept the supernatural Healing God has for us.

Without the fruit of Kindness, we would not be able to use the gift of working of Miracles. The gift of Prophecy is a supernatural disclosure that brings exhortation to the body of Christ. To exhort and edify body of Christ we must first possess the virtues and values of Goodness. Faithfulness is the foundation for being true only to our Lord and is then that we may seek the gift of Discerning of Spirits.

A different kind of tongues is praying or singing in a supernatural or heavenly language. We cannot deliver the message of God if we do not have the fruit of Gentleness. To be Self-control, one must be true and accurate. Interpretation of tongues needs the person of Self Control.

PREFACE

This book is about the fruit of the Spirit in Galatians 5:22-23. The fruit of the Spirit is the character of God growing in the lives of the people who work with His help. To develop and show this fruit we need to learn to be loving, joyful, peaceful, patient, kind, good, faithful, gentle and self-control.

Love which is patient, love which is kind, which does not boast. It is not proud. It is not rude. It is not self-seeking, it is not easily angered. It keeps no record or wrongs. Love does not delight in evil but rejoices with the truth, it always protects, always trust, always hopes, and always preserves. Love never fails.

Joy which is there in heaven when a sinner repents and a repentant sinner also has great joy as if he had found hidden treasure. We must continue to have that joy, whatever the circumstances. Peace which is our Lord Jesus Christ. He made peace by reconciling us to God through His death. We must be peace-makers, not just peace-lovers, as we share the gospel of peace with others.

God sees our suffering and sometimes causes it with good reason and this leads learn and grow if we persevere. Our patience and perseverance can be challenged when dealing with others who may seem rude, stubborn and irritating with negative attitude. Kindness is how we ought to treat each other at all times. Sometimes when we wish to be unkind we must think of God kindness in sending His Son Jesus Christ.

To show goodness in life we need to keep our mind free of selfishness and sinfulness and fill it with good things. Reading the Bible and filling our minds with good things, will lead us to goodness. If we want to be blessed, we must trust God and remain faithful to Him. He will always faithfully care for us if we follow Him.

We must behave in a gentle and kind manner to others because the Word of God in 2 Timothy 2:24-25 says "And the Lord's servant must not quarrel; instead, he must be kind to everyone, able to teach, not resentful. Those who oppose him he must gently instruct, in the hope that God will grant them repentance leading them to knowledge of the truth."

Self-control is the last in the list of the fruit of the Spirit. Each person has some areas – in thought or action – where they find self-control difficult. To enter the kingdom of God we must learn self-control to avoid sin.

TABLE OF CONTENT

Page

INTRODUCTION

Galatians 5:22 (New King James Version) But the fruit of the Spirit is love, joy, peace, longsuffering, kindness, goodness, faithfulness, [23] gentleness, self-control. Against such there is no law.

Galatians 5:22 (New International Reader's Version) But the fruit, the Holy Spirit produces is love, joy and peace. It is being patient, kind and good. It is being faithful [23] and gentle and having control of oneself. There is no law against things of that kind.

Fruit of the spirit is a biblical term that sums up the nine visible attributes of a true Christian life. According to the Bible, these fruits are not ones elected by an individual; rather, the fruit of the Spirit is a single nine fold (fruit) that characterizes all who truly walk in the Holy Spirit. A study of the fruit of the Spirit is a wonderful study, and is important to all Christians at any level of spiritual maturity. This is the fruit that all Christians should be producing in their new lives with Jesus Christ. In nutshell "we MUST BE BORN AGAIN" (John 3:7 NIV). This nine fold fruit comprises the major qualities that are coming direct from God Himself and every Christian should do the best they can to work with the Holy Spirit to produce all nine aspects of the fruit.

Jesus Christ set us free. We are free from slavery, free from bondage, free from strongholds and the rights the devil claims to have on us. The Devil does not have control or a say on our lives unless we listen to him when he whispers in our ears, telling us that we still belong to him. It is the nature of the devil to use our past sins from which our Saviour had actually cleansed us through His blood on the cross of Calvary. Galatians 5:1 "Christ has set us free. He wants us to enjoy freedom. So stand firm. Don't let the chains of slavery hold you again."

Christians must not forget that the devil is a loser but he does not want to be tormented alone in hell. When God threw him out from heaven after he tried to overthrow the kingdom of God, he intended not to go alone into the bottomless pit. That is why he is trying by all means to steal our fruit of the Sprit.

God desires that all Christians enjoy this fruit and have fellowship freely with Him. This book endeavours to help us understand who we are in Christ and why we should enjoy the fruit our Father has planted in us.

Let us pray and ask God to give us revelation knowledge of these: "Dear heavenly Father, I ask You as I enter into this journey of understanding the fruit of the Spirit to help me understand and give the revelation knowledge of what you really have for. Help me to understand and enjoy this fruit. I ask these in the name of our Lord and Saviour Jesus Christ - Amen."

CHAPTER ONE

LOVE: (Latin: *caritas*)

Love is the first of the fruit of the Spirit, the one trait of God that exemplifies His character. John Ritenbaugh explains what love is and what love does: ... Obedience to His commands is godly love, the fruit of His Spirit that empowers us, the supreme virtue of the Almighty our Creator.

The word *love* can mean many different things in the English language. It can refer to a mother's love for her child, love of a country, romantic love, friendship, or God's love towards mankind. The Greek language has different words for different types of love, *agape, eros* and *phileo.*

The word rendered "love" is *agape* in the Greek, which in the Christian context refers to unconditional love. It is the love that God has for His Son and toward mankind. *Agape* denotes an invincible benevolence and unconquerable goodwill that always seek the highest of the other, no matter what he does. It is the self-giving love that gives freely without asking anything in return, and that does not consider the worth of its object. *Agape* is more a love by choice than *phileo*, which is love by chance; and it refers to the will rather than the emotion. *Agape* describes the unconditional love God has for the world. The "Agape" love is more than that; it is sacrificial, as demonstrated by Jesus at the cross of Calvary.

Eros is a sensual sexual love. This is where we get the English word "erotic" from.

Agape love comes only from God. It does not always run with natural inclinations. It gives unselfishly. It takes actions and is visible – you can see it in action. It is ready to serve. It does what is best. It is not drawn out by excellence and it deliberate choice without cause. This is the kind of love from the book of 1 Corinthians 13:4-8

Dear friend, "let us love *(agape)* one another, for love *(agape)* is of God, and everyone who loveth *(agape)* is born of God and knoweth God" (1 John 4:7). Agape love is love that only comes from God. 1 John 4:9-10 "This is how God showed His love **(agape)** among us: He sent His one and only Son into the world that we might live through Him. This is love *(agape);* not that we loved (agape) God but that He loved *(agape)* us and sent His Son as an atoning sacrifice for our sins."

In contrast, *phileo* is defined as to be friend to, indicating feelings, warm affection. *Phileo* is the love that can come easily because of like interests, commonalities. *Phileo* is never used in a command given to men to love God.

1 John 4:16 "And so we know and rely on the love God has for us, God is love. Whoever lives in love lives in God, and God in him." Through Jesus Christ, our greatest goal is to do all things in love. 1 Corinthians 13:4-8 "Love is patient, love is kind. It keeps no record of wrongs. Love does not delight in evil but rejoices with the truth. It always protects, always trusts, always hopes, and always perseveres. Love never fails." Life without love is empty. One cannot imagine being there without love or not being loved.

God's Love towards us, His estranged creation, is graphically depicted in the sacrifice He made on our behalf. John 15:13 "Greater love has no one than this that a man lay down His life for His friends."

Jesus Christ is God's unique and eternal Son. He is the Alpha and Omega, the Beginning and End, the Great I AM, the Mighty God by whom all things were created and in whom all things consist. Jesus, who is the head of all things, humbled Himself in such a way that the human mind could not even bear the thought of it. He came into this sin-cursed world and actively partook in our sufferings. Even as we are flesh and blood, He shared in the same. He became a man and dwelt among us. He shared in the sufferings we had brought upon ourselves through our rejection of His holy precepts. And as if that were not enough to convince us of His love and concern for us, Jesus the immortal God and the Giver of Life, gave up His own life upon the cross in the greatest act of love the world has ever known. In doing so He took our sins away, effectively nailing them to the cross with Himself. Thus, He who knew no sin became sin for us and He who gave life to all, tasted death for those condemned to it.

John 3:16-17 "For God so loved the world that He gave His one and only Son, that whoever believes in Him shall not perish but have eternal life. For God did not send His Son into the world to condemn the world, but to save the world through Him." Jesus Christ loved the world so much that He gave everything for it, from His rights and privileges as the unique eternal Son of God, to His very life. This can be seen from the cross. 1 John 4:9-10 "This is how God showed His love among us; He sent his one and only Son into the world that we might live through Him. This is love: not that we loved God, but that He loved us and sent His Son as an atoning sacrifice for our sins." God wanted all of us to fellowship with Him. Romans 6:23 "For the wages of sin is death, but the gift of God is eternal life in Christ Jesus our Lord." God does not want anybody to die because of sin. By sending His only Son, He wanted everybody on earth to be covered once and for all. This is God's Love.

God created the earth and everything on it with love. There is no way that God would want His creation to perish. God's Love is for us. God's love has been made known to us and now He stands at the door and knocks. It's up to every individual to either pursue a personal relationship with God or else reject Him outright. The only barrier between us and God's love is our own free will, and Jesus Christ is the door. John 14:6 "Jesus answered, I am the way and the truth and the life. No one come to the Father except through me." Only through Jesus Christ can people have eternal life. "WE MUST BE BORN AGAIN" (John 3:7). Salvation is a free gift brought and paid for by the blood of Jesus Christ. Forgiveness cannot be earned through good works.

If we want to see love in action, we must check 1 Corinthians 13:4-10: "Love is patient and kind. Love is not jealous or boastful or proud or rude. It does not demand its own way. It is not irritable, and it keeps no record of being wronged. It does not rejoice about injustice but rejoices whenever the truth wins out. Love never gives up, never loses faith, is always hopeful, and endures through every circumstance. Prophecy and speaking in unknown languages and special knowledge will become useless. But love will last forever! [9] Now our knowledge is partial and incomplete, and even the gift of prophecy reveals only part of the whole picture! But when full understanding comes, these partial things will become useless. Three things will last forever—faith, hope, and love—and the greatest of these is love.

We can fall on our knees and acknowledge God' only provision for our sins. A man once fell on his knees before Christ and begged, Mark 1:40-41: "If You are willing, You can make me clean, Christ, filled with compassion, replied, 'I am willing." Because of love, there no way that Jesus would not be willing to heal the man. If we accept His death upon the cross as payment for our sins, we will be reconciled to the God who we have offended. 2 Corinthians 5:18-19, 21: "All this is from God, who reconciled us to Himself through Christ... God was reconciling the world to Himself in Christ, not counting men's sins against them. God made Him no sin to be sin for us, so that in Him we might become the righteousness of God." It is upon each and every one of us who did not accept this love to accept it today.

Galatians 5:13 "My brothers and sisters, you were chosen to be free. But don't use your freedom as an excuse to live in sin. Instead, serve one another in love. [14] The whole law can be found in a single command." "Do not take revenge or bear a grudge against members of your community but Love your neighbour as you love yourself: I am the Lord" (Leviticus 19:18 NIV). People who normally take revenge are those without love. If you really love your neighbour, even if he does something wrong, you will not take revenge. Let us live with our Lord's command – LOVE and enjoy this fruit.
Galatians 5:24 "Those who belong to Christ Jesus have nailed their sinful nature to his cross. They don't want what their sinful nature loves and longs for. [25] Since we live by the Spirit, let us march in step with the Spirit. [26] Let us not become proud. Let us not make each other angry. Let us not want what belongs to others." Let us love each other.

If animals show love to each other, how much the more should we, who are created in the image of our Father – God. "One day the dog said to the cat – 'Hey man, you see our master does not care about us. Let us show him what love is. He knows very well that I hate you and I cannot stay with you in one place. But this time we must show him that we were also created by God who loves everything He created. Let us go and wait for him at the gate, so that immediately when he arrives, he will see us together.

So the cat and the dog went to wait for their master at the gate, with the cat sleeping on the leg of the dog. Immediately when their master arrived, he saw this picture and he tried to chase them apart, as he knew that they were enemies. Instead, the cat followed the dog into the little doghouse to show their master that they can even stay together. This did something to their master. He was thinking of this picture and he said to his mind that if enemies could stay together with the love one sees in these animals, it means God is working hard to bring us people together. Their master started to think of his enemies and tried to reconcile with them."

You see, God can use anything to help us love one another. "Do not take revenge or bear *a* grudge against members of your community but Love your neighbour as you love yourself: I am the Lord"— *(Leviticus 19:18 NIV).*

God wants us to have unconditional love, the love which is silence – when ours would hurt. The love which is patience – when our neighbours are curt. The love which is deaf- when a scandal flows. The love which thoughtfulness for others' woes. The love that is courageous when misfortune falls. Unconditional love is foundational.

Let us pray: Dear Heavenly Father, thank You for the love you have for us. Help us to develop the very same LOVE so that we can have the character like yours. We are prepared to be your good ambassadors and we need your help. We understand that everything is from you and we ask these in the powerful Name of our Lord Jesus Christ – Amen."

CHAPTER TWO

JOY: (Latin: *gaudium*)

Joy is the second fruit of the Spirit. It is more than just happiness. It is a joy that God gives that far exceeds mere human character. It appears that for us to experience biblical joy, the fruit of God's Spirit, we need godly inner qualities that we do not possess by nature

The Greek word for joy is *chara,* derived from the word *charis,* which is the Greek word for grace. It is important to note that *chara* is produced by *charis* of God. This means joy is not a human-based happiness that comes and goes. Rather, true joy is divine in origin. It is a Spirit-given expression that flourishes best in hard times.

Joy is a sense of delight and well-being. Everybody has joy within them. Joy is always within us, regardless of what may be happening around us. Christ is the only source of believers' joy.

Nehemiah 8:10 "The joy of the Lord is your strength." It means that, without the joy of the Lord, we do not have strength. Joy is one of the things that God can fully restore in every life. Hebrews 12:2 "Let us fix our eyes on Jesus, the author and finisher of our faith, who for the joy that was set before him endured the cross, despising the shame, and is set down at the right hand of the throne of God." God wants us to fix our eyes to Him alone. He wants our joy to be complete. John 15:11 "I have told you this so that my joy may be in you and that you joy may be complete. My command is this: Love each other as I have loved you." This takes us to first fruit of the Spirit Love. For our joy to be complete, God wants us to love each other.

Deuteronomy 16:15 "For seven days celebrate the feast to the Lord your God at the place the Lord will choose. For the Lord your God will bless you in all your harvest and in all the work of your hands, and your joy will be complete." In the first place for our joy to be complete; God must choose the place for enjoyment before and it is then that our joy will be complete. We must wait for the Holy Spirit to direct us to the places where we must be at a specific time. Some of the places we choose for ourselves get us into trouble where we will not have joy. God is the only One who can turn our sorrow into joy.

We cannot have everlasting joy if we do not have Jesus as our Saviour in our hearts. Esther 9:22: "At the time when the Jews got relief from their enemies and as the month when their sorrow turned into joy and their mourning into a day of celebration ..." To be in bondage is something that deprives Christians of the joy of our Lord. We need to be delivered from the spirit of bondage in order to have this joy.

Isaiah 35 talks about the joy of the redeemed. "And the ransomed of the Lord will return. They will enter Zion with singing; everlasting joy will crown their heads. Gladness and joy will overtake them and sorrow and sighing will flee away" (Isaiah 35:10). When the sinner gives his life to God and allows God to control his life, all the spirits that hinder a Christian to have his joy will flee away. Those are the devil's legal rights, bondage and strongholds.

It is easy for our grief to turn into joy. Jesus Christ tells us that He is the truth, the way and the life. If we turn to the way, we will get the truth that will set us free and if we are free will get everlasting life. John 16:20 "I tell you the truth; you will weep and mourn while the world rejoice. You will grieve but your grief will turn into joy." In Jesus Christ, weeping and grieving is temporary. Weeping and grieving are things that we see with our eyes and they are not forever. 2 Corinthians 4:18 "So we fix our eyes not on what is seen, but on what is unseen, for what is seen is temporary, but what is unseen is eternal."

1 Thessalonians 5:16 "Be joyful always; pray continually; give thanks in all circumstances, for this is God's will for you in Christ Jesus." God appeals to us to be joyful at all times and to give thanks in all circumstances. It is not easy to pray continually and give thinks in all circumstances if we do not have Jesus Christ as our Saviour in our hearts. Christ as the Alfa and Omega, beginner and finisher of everything, is the only one to give this joy or rather the fruit of the

Spirit. "Rejoice in the Lord always, I will say it again: Rejoice!" (Philippians 4:4).

It is important that we have some level of God's joy operating through us in this life. Without God's joy operating in our life, things will begin to dry up. We should work very closely with the Holy Spirit in not only getting Him to release His joy into our system, but to also in keeping it running on a regular and consistent basis.

THE CAUSES OF NOT HAVING THE JOY OF GOD

-   **SIN:** This is the greatest stumbling block to our joy, because sin prevents Jesus from filling us with the joy. Sin causes us not to understand who we are in Christ. Sin makes the child of God see everything with a negative eye. King David was the man next to the heart of God, but because of the sin he committed with Uriah's wife Bathsheba, he did not have joy in his heart, until God sent Prophet Nathan to tell him about his sin. We get the whole story in 2 Samuel 11:1-27. King David wrote Psalm 51 after Prophet Nathan had confronted him with the facts: "Restore to me the joy of your salvation and grant me a willing spirit, to sustain me." (Psalm 51:12).

    Sin is a terrible thing, and it robs us of our joy. It also affects our Christian ways. We cannot walk with our God if we still have some of the things that hinder our Lord to work in us. Until we surrender our lives completely to our Lord Jesus Christ, we will not have the complete joy that God wants us to have.

-   **MISPLACED CONFIDENCE**: We need to be contended, we must realize that God is in total control of our lives including our jobs, our families, our finances, our blessings, our plans, etc. "For I know the plans I have for you, declares the LORD, plans to prosper you and not to harm you, plans to give you hope and a future" (Jeremiah 29:11). It is important not to put our confidence in the flesh, because we will find ourselves anxious, tense, struggling, tired and disappointed. Our God is forever good. He does not change. He is there for us. He promised us not leave us nor forsake us.

18

We must put our trust in the Lord. Psalm 37:3 "Trust in the Lord and do good; dwell in the land and enjoy safe pasture. Delight yourself in the Lord and He will give you the desires of your heart." "Trust in the Lord with your heart and lean not on your own understanding" (Proverbs 3:5). "Whoever trusts in his riches will fall, but the righteous will thrive like a green leaf" (Proverbs 11:28). "He who trust in himself is a fool, but he who walks with wisdom is kept safe" (Proverbs 28:26). We must not forget that wisdom comes from God. God is our only trust. In order to be contended and to have joy, our confidence must be in Christ alone. WE "MUST BE BORN AGAIN" (John 3:7).

- **WRONG ATTITUDES TOWARDS GOD'S DISCIPLINE**: Hebrews 12:6 "My son, do not make light of the Lord's discipline, and do not lose heart when He rebukes you, because the Lord disciplines those He loves, and he punishes everyone He accepts as a son." We must accept the discipline of our God because He loves us. God knows our thought and He does not want us to live our lives in a way that will take us to hell. Psalm 94: 11-13 "The Lord knows the thoughts of man; He knows that they are futile. Blessed is the man You discipline, O Lord; the man You teach from your law, you grant him relief from days of trouble."

God disciplines us because He loves us. Revelation 3:19 "Those whom I love, I rebuke and discipline. So be earnest and repent." When we look at the world, sometimes it is tough for a child to accept the discipline of someone outside the family, someone who is not his parent. But if the father disciplines his child, he shows love, and the father will try to build a better future for the child. This is the same as our heavenly Father. He disciplines us because we are His sons and daughters. It is not easy for us to accept discipline, unless we know our Lord and Saviour. To know Him, "WE MUST BE BORN AGAIN" (John 3:7).

- **GROWING WEARY DURING TRIALS OF FAITH**: The purpose of trials is to exercise our faith, so that we can grow spiritually and become strong. Trials are the same as discipline.

Discipline deals with sin in our lives. God allows trails to come into our lives for his purpose, to strengthen our faith and to build character, so that we can be used by God. James 1:2-3 "Consider it pure joy, my brothers, whenever you face trials of many kinds. Because you know that the testing of your faith develops perseverance."

It is important to stay focused and be like Job when he found that he had lost all of his earthly possessions as well as his children. Job did not lose sight, he stayed focused. Job 1:21 "Naked I came from my mother's womb, and naked I will depart. The Lord gave and the Lord has taken away, may the name of the Lord be praised." Sometimes if we lose what we accumulated on earth, we forget that we are not of the world. 1 John 2:15-17 "Do not love the world or anything in the world. If anyone loves the world, the love of the Father is not in him. For everything in the world- the cravings of sinful and, the lust of his eyes and the boasting of what he has and does – comes not from the Father but from the world. The world and its desires pass will away, but the man who does the will of God lives forever." God remained faithful and stayed with Job until Job learned of God's sovereignty. It is not the intention of God to give up on us. Hence disciplines and trials. God blessed Job with twice as much as he had lost. "After Job had prayed for his friends, the Lord prospered him again and gave him twice as much as he had before" (Job 42:10). During the trials there will be people who will discourage you in the way of the Lord. Some will advise you to leave God and try other ways which they think are better ways than the way of the Lord. People like the statement that says "God helps those who help themselves." God wants us to pray for people like them as Job did. We must not forget that some of them will be our enemies and God wants us to love them. Matthew 5:44-45 "But I tell you: Love you enemies and pray for those who persecute you, that you may be sons of your Father in heaven."

GETTING THE JOY OF GOD

Joy comes from God. We are responsible to exhibit joy in our lives and to depend on the Holy Spirit for the power to exhibit the joy that God has given to us. "May the God of hope fill you with all joy and peace as you trust in Him, so that you may overflow with hope by the power of the Holy Spirit." We cannot have the joy of the Lord if we still have sins in our lives. We should be willing to obey God and resist the temptation of sin.

- **CONFESSION OF SINS:** David, the man next to the heart of God was always willing to repent and confess his sins. "Then I acknowledge my sin to you and did not cover up my iniquity, I said 'I will confess my transgression to the Lord and you forgave the guilt of my sin. If we confess our sins, God is good enough to forgive us.

    The Bible states that we are all sinners, "For all have sinned and fall short of the glory of God" (Romans 3:23). Because of this we must confess our sins to God. Romans 10:9 "That if you confess with your mouth "Jesus is Lord," and believe in you heart that God rose from the dead, you will be saved."

    God is faithful enough to purify us and give us the joy we deserve. "If we confess our sins, He is faithful and just, and will forgive us our sins and purify us from all unrighteousness" (1 John 1:9).

- **TRUST GOD:** We cannot trust in God if we do not accept Him in our hearts. God cannot work in us or use us if we are not born again. God cannot fill us with joy if we do not trust Him. "May the God of hope fill you with all joy and peace as you trust in Him, so that you may overflow with hope by the power of the Holy Spirit" (Romans 15:13).

    Psalm 37:3 "Trust in the Lord and do good; dwell in the land and enjoy safe pasture. Delight yourself in the Lord and He will give you the desires of your heart." "Trust in the Lord with your heart and lean not on your own understanding" (Proverbs 3:5). "Whoever trusts in his riches will fall, but the righteous will thrive like a green leaf" (Proverbs 11:28). "He who trust in himself is a fool, but he who walks with wisdom is kept safe" (Proverbs 28:26).

God controls everything on earth. Romans 8:28 "And we know that in all things God works for the good of those who love Him, who have been called according to His purpose." God wants us to come to the point where we trust Him without questioning anything.

- **HOLDING ON TO THE ETERNAL INHERITANCE:** Deuteronomy 4:20 "But the Lord selected you and brought you out of Egypt's iron furnace to be a people for His inheritance, as you are today." Our Lord is not a person. He cannot lie. If He said He wants us to be His inheritance, He means it, and it is important for us to hold on to that. We must "fix our eyes to Jesus, the author and perfecter of our faith, who for the joy set before him endured the cross, scorning its shame, and sat down at the right hand of the throne of God." (Hebrews 12:2).

- **GIVE THANKS:** Our Lord is our Father, our Protector during troubles, our Defender, our Provider, Our Guide, and He is everything to us. We must always give thanks to Him. He our Omnipotent God, Omnipresent and Omniscient. He knows all our situations. He wants our relationship with Him to be perfect so that we can be His inheritance. 2 Chronicles 16:8 "Give thanks to the Lord; call on His Name; proclaim His Deeds among the people." People must know the great and good things our Lord is doing for us. 2 Thessalonians 5:18: "Give thanks in everything, for this is God's will for you in Christ Jesus."

If we do not know where our inheritance is located or based, we will travel the entire world and will not find where we belong. "One man wanted to get rich and thought that it would make him happy or that it would give him the joy forever. He first thought 'if I get educated, I will be famous and everybody will know, and I will be happy.' Then he studied to the highest qualification one can think of. He was famous, but he did not have joy in his heart.

He thought again of getting a highly paid job and that if he could buy anything he wanted, he would be happy. Because of his high qualifications he got a highly paid job and he could buy expensive and luxurious things. But he was not yet happy. He did not have joy.

Then one day while he was travelling on a plane, he met a guy who sat next to him. Actually they were travelling to the same overseas destination. He was going to attend a business meeting while the other guy was attending a church conference. The highly qualified man was reading a magazine while the other man was reading the bible.

The man who was reading the magazine come across the column that said a rich and highly qualified man killed himself because he thought he had everything he wanted and he does not need anything on earth. The article went on to say he also killed his family because he did not want them to enjoy his riches while he was away.

The man reading the Bible come across the Scriptures that says: Psalm 37:3 "Trust in the Lord and do good; dwell in the land and enjoy safe pasture. Delight yourself in the Lord and He will give you the desires of your heart." "Trust in the Lord with your heart and lean not on your own understanding." (Proverbs 3:5). "Whoever trusts in his riches will fall, but the righteous will thrive like a green leaf" (Proverbs 11:28). "He who trust in himself is a fool, but he who walks with wisdom is kept safe" (Proverbs 28:26).
The man reading the magazine responded aloud and said, "hoo, stupid man, didn't he know that when you have money you have everything." The man who was reading the Bible looked at him and said, "maybe the poor man did not use his money to buy joy or he did not know the supermarket where joy is sold." The rich man looked at him and said, "that is what I am looking for too; where this supermarket is?"

The man reading the Bible looked at him and showed him the Bible and read to him Psalm 37:3 "Trust in the Lord and do good; dwell in the land and enjoy safe pasture. Delight yourself in the Lord and He will give you the desires of your heart." "Trust in the Lord with your heart and lean not on your own understanding" (Proverbs 3:5). "Whoever trusts in his riches will fall, but the righteous will thrive like a green leaf" (Proverbs 11:28). "He who trust in himself is a fool, but he who walks with wisdom is kept safe" (Proverbs 28:26).

The man was sad and he asked the man who was reading the Bible where he was going because he needed to be with him to understand all these things Miraculously the business meeting he was going to attend was going to be next to the church where the conference would be held. The rich man was invited to the conference, and at the conference the preacher preached from Romans 15:13 "May the God of hope fill you with all joy and peace as you trust in Him, so that you may overflow with hope by the power of the Holy Spirit."

There is no supermarket for joy; God is the provider of all our needs.

Let us pray "Dear heavenly Father, Grant me the joy that comes from You, because You are our only Source of Happiness. Give the joy that will help me to glorify you, the joy that will help me and make me your true vessel. I am asking this in the miracle-working Name of our Lord, Jesus Christ. Amen."

CHAPTER THREE

PEACE: (Latin: *pax*)

Peace comes from the Greek word *eirene*, the Geek equivalent for the Hebrew word *shalom*, which expresses the idea of wholeness, completeness, or tranquillity in the soul that is unaffected by the outward circumstances or pressures. Peace is the result of resting in a relationship with God. Peace is tranquillity, the state of rest that comes from seeking God.

Peace is not the absence of conflict, but the presence of God, no matter what the conflict."

Isaiah 9:6 "For to us a child is born, to us a son is given, and the government will on his shoulder. And He will be called *Wonderful Counsellor*, *Mighty God*, *Everlasting Father*, and *Prince of Peace*." To have this Peace, we must accept the Prince of Peace in our hearts. Because He is the Prince of Peace, He said in John 14:27, "Peace I leave with you; my peace I give you. I do not give to you as the world gives. Do not let your hearts be troubled and do not be afraid." Peace has nothing to do with circumstances but everything to do with knowing our God.

By enjoying peace in this world, this does not mean that we will not have troubles in this world. John 16:3 "I have told you these things, so that in me you have overcome the world." Sometimes we forget about the peace we have in God, because we get distracted by the troubles of this world. It is a question of focus. We must check whether we are focused on the troubles of this world or the peace of God. Christ overcame what the world had to offer when He chose to die for us on the cross. Romans 5:18-19 "Consequently, just as the result of one trespass was condemnation for all men, so also the result of one act of righteousness was justification that brings life for all men. For just as through the disobedience of the one man the many were made sinners, so also through the obedience of one man the many will be made righteous."

Romans 5:1, 13 "Therefore, since we have been justified through faith, we have peace with God through our Lord Jesus Christ." "May the God of hope fill joy and peace as you trust in Him, so that you may overflow with hope by the power of the Holy Spirit." Jesus made it clear to us that "I have told you these things so that in Me you may have peace. You will have sufferings in this world. Be courageous! I have conquered the world." Jesus conquered the world and its troubles. It is for us to take into consideration that the troubles of this world must not take the peace our Lord left for us. The devil is a thief, and a thief can steal anything, even things we may not consider valuable. We must not allow the thief – Devil to steal our inheritance.

Peace requires an intense effort because:

- We still live in earthly bodies which require us to choose each day who we will serve. Even though we were saved by God's grace and are a part of the family of God, we still have to make a conscious decision each day as to whether we will serve God or chase after what the world has to offer. We should understand that we do not belong to the world - John15:19 "If you were of this world, the world would love you as its own. However, because you are not of the world, but I have chosen you out of it, the world hates you."

How do we find peace in the midst of all the distractions?

- Isaiah 9:6 "For to us a child is born, to us a son is given, and the government will on his shoulder. And He will be called *Wonderful Counsellor*, *Mighty God*, *Everlasting Father*, and *Prince of Peace*." The first place to find peace is in Christ through receiving Him as our Lord and Saviour, because Jesus is the Prince of Peace. Romans 5:1-2 "Therefore, since we have been justified through faith, we have peace with God through our Lord Jesus Christ, through whom we have gained access by faith into this grace in which we now stand."

- Galatians 5:25 "Since we live by the Spirit, let us keep in step with the Spirit." So we choose daily to crucify the flesh with its passions and desires and we choose God's way. We walk by the Spirit; we set our minds on the Spirit. It is important for us to submit to God's law at all times. Romans 8:6-7 "The mind of sinful man is death, but the mind controlled by the Spirit is life and peace; the sinful mind is hostile to God. It does not submit to God's law, nor can it do so."

- Trust God and take Him at His Word:

  - Joshua 1:9 "Have I not commanded you? Be strong and courageous. Do not be terrified; do not be discouraged, for the Lord you God will be with you whenever you go."
  - Lamentations 3:22-23 "Because of the Lord's great love we are not consumed, for his compassions never fail. They are new every morning; great is your faithfulness."
  - 1 John 4:4 "You, dear children, are from God and have overcome them, because the one who is in you is greater than the one who is in the world."
  - Romans 8:28 "And we know that in all things God works for the good of those who love Him, who have been called according to His purpose."
  - Romans 8:31 "What, then, shall we say in response to this? If God is for us, who can be against us?"
  - Romans 8:38-39 "For I am convinced that neither death nor life, neither angels not demons, neither the present nor the future, nor any powers, neither height nor depth, not anything else in all creation, will be able to separate us form the love of God that is in Christ Jesus our Lord."
  - 2 Corinthians 12:9 "But He said to me, 'My grace is sufficient for you, for my power is made perfect in weakness.' Therefore I will boast all the more gladly about my weaknesses, so that Christ's power may rest on me."
  - Philippians 4:6-7 "Do not be anxious about anything, but in everything, by prayer and petition, with thanksgiving, present your requests to God. And the peace of God,

which transcends all understanding, will guard your hearts and your minds in Christ Jesus."
- Philippians 4:13 " I can do everything through Him who gives me strength."
- Philippians 4:19 "And my God will meet all you needs according to his glorious riches in Christ Jesus."
- 1 Peter 5:7 "Cast all you anxiety on Him, because He cares for you."

If we check out the scriptures above, we can see that God's mercies are good daily. Our God knows our hearts, our plans, and our needs. He is prepared to bless us and to supply in the needs we desire. We must be courageous in everything we do, no matter where life takes us every day, no matter what type of troubles we experience; because we have the Price of Peace in our hearts, the peace is ours. When we come to Him in prayer and thanksgiving, He promises peace that surpasses all understanding. We must choose to accept that promise and to take God at His Word. We must appropriate that peace in our lives, and we must examine our lives to see what is causing us anxiety or worry or loss of contentment. Whenever we identify an area in our lives that is causing anxiety or worry, we must confess it to God in prayer and then apply God's peace to that specific area in our lives.

The quality of peace should be one of the main qualities that we should try and get worked up into our soul through the Holy Spirit in the sanctification process. Without the peace of god operating in our lives, we could become very easily rattled, shaken, tormented, and knocked right off of our game in the Lord the first time any adversity should ever come our way.

When the Lord looks at us, He always wants to give us a great favour and peace. Numbers 6:26 "The Lord looks with favour on you and gives you peace." We must seek peace and pursue it. Psalm 34:14 "Turn away from evil and do what is good; seek peace and pursue it."

28

One man once said "I want to have peace of mind; I want to be alone in a quiet place where no one can see or talk to me." Then he left and went to the place where he thought no man or anything else would be. On his way; there was lot of things in his mind. He was thinking of his debts, his children, his family members his colleagues and all other things. He did not once think about God, however, because he did not know Him. When he arrived where he wanted to be; his mind was already tired, and he had to go on with his thinking of all those things. He spent the time there alone, but his mind was still on duty.

When it was time to go back, he was more tired than when he went away. Then he was wondering what the use was of being alone. The problem was that he had missed it somewhere. Whatever we do; we must do it with the owner of everything. If we want peace, we must know the Prince of Peace. If we want counselling; we must seek the Wonderful Counsellor. We cannot have peace if we reject the Prince of peace.

Let us pray: Dear heavenly Father, we come before You our Prince of Peace, because we need peace that is from You. In all the situations; You are the only one who can counsel us and put us in the right positions. Help us dear Lord, to take things the way You want us to take them. Open our ears so that we can hear good things, open our eyes so that we can see perfect things and please reveal to us your knowledge, in Jesus' Name, Amen.

CHAPTER FOUR

LONGSUFFERING (PATIENCE): (Latin: *longanimitas*)

This is defined in several terms as follows:
- The bearing of provocation, annoyance, misfortune, pain, etc., without complaint, loss of temper or irritation.
- An ability or willingness to suppress annoyance when confronted with delay.
- Quiet perseverance; even-tempered care; diligence.

Let us consider the following Scriptures:
James 1:2-4 "Consider it pure joy my brothers, whenever you face trails of many kinds, because you know that the testing of your faith develops perseverance. Perseverance must finish its work so that you may be mature and complete, not lacking anything."

James 5:10-11 "Be patient, then brothers, until the Lord's coming. See how the farmer waits for the land to yield its valuable crop and how patient he is for the autumn and spring rains. You too, be patient and stand firm, because the Lord's coming is near."

2 Peter 1:5-9 "For this reason, make every effort to add to your faith goodness; and to goodness, knowledge; and to knowledge, self-control; and to self-control, perseverance; and to perseverance, godliness; and to godliness, brotherly kindness; and to brotherly kindness, love. For if you possess these qualities in increasing measure, they will keep you from being ineffective and unproductive in your knowledge of our Lord Jesus Christ. But if anyone does not have them, he is near-sighted and blind, and has forgotten that he has been cleansed from his past sins."

Colossians 1:11 "We are strengthened with might, according to his glorious power, unto all patience and longsuffering with joyfulness." "With all lowliness and meekness, with longsuffering, forbearing one another in love" (Ephesians 4:2).

Job is the good example of man of longsuffering. Though he was sinless, he got into the severe trials and tribulations so that all his friends would question his kindness. His strong belief in God resulted in a deep respect for God and consequently he shunned evil. It is important in our lives that God trust us in a way that He can send the devil to tempt us. Job's moral character was upright. The book of Job shows us that Satan does not give-up easily. The Devil will keep on tormenting us until we give-up. It important for us to consider the Scriptures that tell us about longsuffering and how good God is. God is able to deal with everybody and everything in a suitable way.

We must learn to ride flow with the patience of the Holy Spirit in our daily lives and to walk with the Lord – and we will then be able to enter into a much more restful and peaceful state of mind and emotion.

We must not think that God is slow in doing things or in answering our prayers. God wants everybody to repent. He does not want anybody to perish. 2 Peter 3:9 "The Lord is not slow in keeping His promise, as some understand slowness. He is patient with you, not wanting anyone to perish, but wants everyone to come to repentance,"

His patience should be interpreted as an opportunity for salvation. 2 Peter 3:15 "Bear in mind that our Lord's patience means salvation, just as our dear brother Paul also wrote you with the wisdom that God gave him." His kindness is meant to lead us toward repentance. Romans 2:4 "Or do you show contempt for the riches of His kindness, tolerance and patience, not realizing that God's kindness leads you toward repentance?" It is not the intentions of God for His people to perish.

We have Bible people who were shown mercy of salvation. For example; Paul the worst of sinners. 1 Timothy 1:16 "But for that very reason I was shown mercy so that in me, the worst of sinners, Christ Jesus might display His unlimited patience as an example for those who would believe in him and receive eternal life." The story of Paul is in Acts chapter 9.

It is our obligation to be patient. We are given command to be patient. "With all lowliness and meekness, with longsuffering, forbearing one another in love" (Ephesians 4:2). We must clothe ourselves with patience. Colossians 3:12 "Therefore as God's chosen people, holy and dearly loved, clothe yourselves with compassion, kindness, humility, gentleness and patience." We must be patient with everyone. 1 Thessalonians 5:14 "And we urge you, brothers, warn those who are idle, encourage the timid, help the weak, be patient with everyone."

We must encourage those who are suffering in trials. They must be patient because the Lord is near. James 5:7-8 "Be patient, then brothers, until the Lord's coming. See how the farmer waits for the land to yield its valuable crop and how patient he is for the autumn and spring rains. You too, be patient and stand firm, because the Lord's coming is near."

Leaders must perform their duties with patience. 2 Timothy 4:2 "Preach the Word, be prepared in season and out of season; correct, rebuke and encourage with great patience and careful instruction." In performing their duties, leaders come across many people of different characters, of which some the characters need patience. Leaders must correct these people, rebuke and encourage them with patience.

We must have patience if we expect God to forgive us. Just as God has been patient with us with the way we lived our lives, we must also be patient with Him. "I am so grateful that God was patient with me because after I accepted Lord Jesus Christ as my personal Lord and Saviour when I was sixteen years old, I slid back and lived a life I do not want to think of today. I am so thankful because God was patient with me until I gave back my life to Him again. I used to cry for the time I wasted when I was not serving Him." But because God is our real Father, He is waiting for us patiently to come back to Him and fellowship with Him. God want to cure us of backsliding. Jeremiah 3:22 "Return, faithless people, I will cure you of backsliding."

Abraham, our forefather is a good example for us to follow or imitate for his patience. God does not want us to be lazy. Hebrews 6:12 "We do not want you to become lazy, but to imitate those who through faith and patience inherit what has been promised." In our case, God promised us eternal life. We must wait patiently for our Christ to come back to us, as the time is near.

If we need patience and have become convinced that we need it, God will most likely bring circumstances in to our lives that will provide the opportunity for our patience to be increased. We must be prepared for such times before they arrive, and we will be better equipped for them. We must study the Word of God, meditate on the Word, pray without ceasing, love our brothers and our enemies, show mercy to everybody, and serve everybody as we would serve God.

I like the Scripture of Matthew 25:31-46 (New King James Version)

[31] "When the Son of Man comes in His glory, and all the holy angels with Him, then He will sit on the throne of His glory. [32] All the nations will be gathered before Him, and He will separate them one from another, as a shepherd divides *his* sheep from the goats. [33] And He will set the sheep on His right hand, but the goats on the left. [34] Then the King will say to those on His right hand, 'Come, you blessed of My Father, inherit the kingdom prepared for you from the foundation of the world: [35] for I was hungry and you gave Me food; I was thirsty and you gave Me drink; I was a stranger and you took Me in; [36] I *was* naked and you clothed Me; I was sick and you visited Me; I was in prison and you came to Me.'

[37] "Then the righteous will answer Him, saying, 'Lord, when did we see You hungry and feed *You,* or thirsty and give *You* drink? [38] When did we see You a stranger and take *You* in, or naked and clothe *You?* [39] Or when did we see You sick, or in prison, and come to You?' [40] And the King will answer and say to them, 'Assuredly, I say to you, inasmuch as you did *it* to one of the least of these My brethren, you did *it* to Me.'

[41] "Then He will also say to those on the left hand, 'Depart from Me, you cursed, into the everlasting fire prepared for the devil and his angels: [42] for I was hungry and you gave Me no food; I was thirsty

and you gave Me no drink; [43] I was a stranger and you did not take Me in, naked and you did not clothe Me, sick and in prison and you did not visit Me.'

[44] "Then they also will answer Him, saying, 'Lord, when did we see You hungry or thirsty or a stranger or naked or sick or in prison, and did not minister to You?' [45] Then He will answer them, saying, 'Assuredly, I say to you, inasmuch as you did not do *it* to one of the least of these, you did not do *it* to Me.' [46] And these will go away into everlasting punishment, but the righteous into eternal life."

When it comes to the situation where I have to help someone; I think of the above scripture and become blessed that I am helping my Lord. There are many ways to serve God as mentioned above. Sometime we think of longsuffering as being in trials but at the same; there are trials where we are to carry our fellow brothers, to feed them, to cloth them, to take care of them and to comfort them. It needs patience to do that. It is only God who can help us to be patient enough.

Let us pray: "Dear heavenly Father, we know that you are the Father of everything. Al things we created by You. For us to be able to handle all situations; we need You. We thank You for being there for us in all circumstances and we ask You, God, to strengthen us in all circumstances. We are asking these in the Name of our Lord and Saviour; Jesus Christ – Amen."

CHAPTER FIVE

GENTLENESS (MEEKNESS):

Gentleness has been explained in the following ways by number of notable men of God:

- "Mildness in dealing with other. Gentleness displays a sensitive regard of others" (Billy Graham).
- "Gentleness is an active trait describing them manner in which we should treat others." (Jerry Bridges) It is the grace which pervades the whole nature, mellowing all which would be harsh. Likened to the harmlessness of a dove.
- meekness is a passive trait describing the proper Christian response when others mistreat us.

Both gentleness & meekness are born of power, not weakness.

Gentleness of Christ is described in Matthew 11:28-30 "Come to me, all you who are weary and burdened, and I will give you rest. Take my yoke upon you and learn from me, for I am gentle and humble in heart, and you will find rest for your souls. For my yoke is easy and my burden is light." There is no better time like to receive the gentleness of Christ than when were burdened, heavy laden, weighted down by life's pressures (demand of family, job, debts, financial problems, not enough time in the day, etc.). Our Lord wants our souls to have rest. The rest that our Lord promises is the inner tranquillity.

Meekness: This refers to the passive way we respond to others when we are mistreated. Meekness is accepting God's dealing with us, considering them as good in that they enhance the closeness of our relationship with Him. Meekness does not blame God for the persecutions and evil doings of men. Meekness wants us to treat others well. To take them as our brothers in love. Colossians 3:12 says "Therefore as God's chosen people, holy and dearly loved, clothe yourselves with compassion, kindness, humility, gentleness and patience." This Scriptures state clearly that we are chosen people of God, who are holy and dearly loved, if we are dearly

35

loved, we must also love other. We cannot have love without compassion, kindness, humility, gentleness and patience, unless we are pretenders.

Galatians 6:1(KJV) "Brethren, if a man be overtaken in a fault, ye which are spiritual, restore such a one in the spirit of meekness; considering thyself, lest thou also be tempted." "With all lowliness and meekness, with longsuffering, forbearing one another in love" (Ephesians 4:2KJV).

Galatians 6:1(NIV)"Brothers, if someone is caught in a sin, you who are spiritual should restore him gently. But watch yourself, or you also may be tempted." Our Lord is a forgiving God. If we want to be like Him, we must also be forgiving. By the blood of Jesus Christ, our sins were forgiven and atoned. That is how we should live with our fellow brothers. We are not to condemn others. We are not to act like the god of this world, the Devil, by condemning our brothers.

2 Timothy 2:24-26: "And the Lord's servant must not quarrel; instead, he must be kind to everyone, able to teach, not resentful. Those who oppose him, he must gently instruct, in the hope that God will grant them repentance leading them to a knowledge of the truth, and that they will come to their senses and escape from the trap of the devil, who has taken them captive to do his will." God wants us to be humbled, to represent Him well on earth. We must not bring shame to the name of our Lord. When we teach our fellow brothers we must not be resentful, we must oppose others in a gentle manner and a way that God will grant repentance to them. We must not forget that only the Holy Spirit is the one to change a person. God is the only to change the hard heart into the humble heart.

1 Peter 3:15-16: But in your hearts set apart Christ as Lord. Always be prepared to give an answer to everyone who asks you to give the reason for the hope that you have. But do this with gentleness and respect, keeping a clear conscience, so that those who speak maliciously against your good behaviour on Christ may be ashamed of their slander." When we live in a way Christ wants us to live, there is not going to be easy for people to slander about us. Our

characters will prove them wrong and that is what Christ wants from us.

2 Corinthians 5:6-7 - We should "In purity, understanding, patience and kindness: in the Holy Spirit and in sincere love; in truthful speech and in the power of God; with weapons of righteousness in the right hand and in the left."

Jesus Christ was a good example of meekness. In His last hours before He died, He used a young donkey to travel to Jerusalem. He did not choose to ride on the expensive transport of his day. But He chose to use a donkey showing gentleness and meekness.

In the garden of Gethsemane, some miraculous things happened that could have caused Him to act differently, but somehow, He just remained gentle. Judas betrayed Him, and even though He knew this, He gave him go ahead for doing what was going to happen. Even during his last hours, displaying meekness, he healed the soldier whose ear was cut off by Peter.

He was falsely accused by the chief priests, His face was spit in, and he was beaten, but He did not fight back. When He was beaten, He could feel all the pains we feel, because He was in the flesh. He was meek and committed to the will of God the Father.

He was mocked by Herod and his soldiers. Pilate ordered that Jesus be flogged with a whip and then crucified. His skin was cut by this whip as it had stones attached to it at the end. The crown of thorns was put on His head and the soldiers nailed Him on the cross. His clothes were divided among them while He was bleeding and dying on the cross. People who mocked Him were saying, "let Him save Himself as He has been saving others." Even while nailed to the cross, Jesus was still gentle to one of the thieves He was crucified with. When the thief ask Him to remember him when He came to His Kingdom, Jesus answered him, "I tell you the truth, today you will be with me in paradise" (Luke 23"23…). Jesus Christ chose to die for everybody even those who mocked and nailed Him to the cross. He willingly laid down His life for others, the ultimate sacrifice. He chose to stay on the cross, for our sins for our good, so that we could be saved. Jesus had a humble heart, He was committed to accepting upon Himself our Father's will. By dying on the cross, accepting upon Himself the punishment that we deserved, He accomplished the Father's will and glorified God the Father.

Whatever we do, we must do to glorify God. By treating others well and responding in a meek manner when we are mistreated, our Father is glorified. We must always pray that our God help us to glorify Him in everything we do. We must ask the Holy Spirit to help us be aware of the situations in which we fail to act with gentleness or concern for others, and also when we fail to exhibit meekness. We must be sensitive to the feelings of others and to the Holy Spirit, because the Holy Spirit is gentle and He is with us at all times. He teaches and reminds us of all good things Jesus taught us. We must not be stubborn when the Holy Spirit guides us. We must prayerfully seek God's guidance and strength in the areas where we fail. Jesus Christ never failed us and He will not let us fail.

We must not think that if people mistreat us and we are gentle and even accept them in a friendly manner, we are fools and useless or we cannot cope in this world. Jesus Christ overcame everything for us. He handled all bad treatment and problems. We must be His good ambassadors. People may think of us as stepladders to their best positions, but God has best positions for His children.

For us to be gentle and meek towards other people, we must have the Prince of Peace, the Wonderful Counsellor, in us. It is a very practical principle: if one has inner peace, one will be gentle to others. When Jesus Christ enters into our hearts, He makes a big change, He transforms us, and because the Holy Spirit is holy, sweet, and gentle, there is no way that one can acquire an unwholesome character, and one does not change.

Sometime when the situations are not the way we expected, we must not act roughly, because we will destroy other things. To be gentle sometimes helps us and saves us. Acting in a gentle and meek manner saves us from sinning. In Numbers 22, we read about Balaam and his donkey.

Numbers 22:21: "So the next morning Balaam got up, saddled his donkey, and started off with the Moabite officials. ²² But God was angry that Balaam was going, so he sent the angel of the Lord to stand in the road to block his way. As Balaam and two servants were riding along, ²³ Balaam's donkey saw the angel of the Lord standing in the road with a drawn sword in his hand. The donkey bolted off the road into a field, but Balaam beat it and turned it back onto the road. ²⁴ Then the angel of the Lord stood at a place where the road narrowed between two vineyard walls. ²⁵ When the donkey saw the angel of the Lord, it tried to squeeze by and crushed Balaam's foot against the wall. So Balaam beat the donkey again. ²⁶ Then the angel of the Lord moved farther down the road and stood in a place too narrow for the donkey to get by at all. ²⁷ This time when the donkey saw the angel, it lay down under Balaam. In a fit of rage Balaam beat the animal again with his staff.

²⁸ Then the Lord gave the donkey the ability to speak. "What have I done to you that deserves your beating me three times?" it asked Balaam.

²⁹ "You have made me look like a fool!" Balaam shouted. "If I had a sword with me, I would kill you!" ³⁰ "But I am the same donkey you have ridden all your life," the donkey answered. "Have I ever done anything like this before?" "No," Balaam admitted.

³¹ Then the Lord opened Balaam's eyes, and he saw the angel of the Lord standing in the roadway with a drawn sword in his hand. Balaam bowed his head and fell face down on the ground before him.

³² "Why did you beat your donkey those three times?" the angel of the Lord demanded. "Look, I have come to block your way because you are stubbornly resisting me. ³³ Three times the donkey saw me and shied away; otherwise, I would certainly have killed you by now and spared the donkey." ³⁴ Then Balaam confessed to the angel of the Lord, **"I have sinned.** I didn't realize you were standing in the road to

block my way. I will return home if you are against my going."

We must pray God to help us not to sin by not acting gently and in a meek way.

Let us pray: Dear heavenly Father, forgive us for retaliating when people mistreat us. Help us to accept all the situations when they come to us. Help us to have the type of love you have for us so that we can treat others they you are treating them. Help us to always say Lord forgive them because they do not know what they are doing. We are asking these in the Name of our Lord and Saviour – Jesus Christ; Amen.

CHAPTER SIX

GOODNESS AND KINDNESS : (Latin word for kindness is *benignitas* and Latin word for goodness is *bonitas*)

The word *kindness* comes from the Greek word *chrestotes,* which meant to show kindness or to be friendly to others, and the term often depicted rulers, governors, or people who were kind, mild and benevolent to their subjects. Kindness is doing something and not expecting anything in return. Kindness is respect and helping others without waiting for someone to help you back. An example of kindness can be found in Ephesians 4:32, where Paul Exhorts us to "be kind (chrestoi) to one another."

Kindness exists perfectly in God. God's kindness is also shown through His provision for our material needs. In Matthew 6:25-35 God shows His kindness by promising us not to worry about our next day and everything else. "Therefore I tell you, do not worry about your life, what you will eat or drink; or about your body, what you will wear. Is not life more important than food, and the body more important than clothes? Look at the birds of the air; they do not sow or reap or store away in barn, and yet your heavenly Father feeds them. Are you not much more valuable than they? Who of you by worrying can add a single hour to his life? And why do you worry about clothes? See how the lilies of the field grow. They do not labour or spin. Yet I tell you that not even Solomon in his entire splendour was dressed like one of these. If that is how God clothes the grass of the field, which is here today and tomorrow is thrown into the fire; will He not much more clothe you. O you of little faith? So do not worry, saying, what shall we eat? Or what shall we drink? Or what shall we war? For the pagans run after all these things, and your heavenly Father knows that you need them. But seek first the Kingdom and His righteousness, and all these things will be given to you as well. Therefore do not worry about tomorrow, for tomorrow will worry about itself. Each day has enough trouble of its own."

God is not just concerned about our physical needs; He is also concerned about our spiritual being. He accepts us even after we had been rebellious. Before some of us can accept Him as our personal Lord and Saviour, we strike first. God is patient with us in our everyday lives. The kindness of God is the reason why He sent his only Son to die for us.

Goodness is moral excellence; virtue; generosity; the activity calculated to advance kindness (this is the doing). Kindness is having a good or benevolent nature or disposition; desiring to do good to others; the sincere desire for the happiness of others (this is the thinking). Kindness is the sincere desire for the happiness of others. Acts 14:17 "…He has shown kindness by giving you rain from heaven and crops in their seasons, He provides you with plenty food and fills you hearts with joy." From this Scripture we can see that it is the desire of our God that we be happy. Hence kindness is the desire for happiness of others.

Goodness is the activity calculated to advance that happiness. Kindness is the thinking, thinking of others. Goodness is the doing. Luke 6:35 "But love your enemies, do good to them, and lend to them without expecting to get anything back. Then your reward will be great, and you will be sons of the Most High, because He is kind to the ungrateful and wicked." God wants us to be His imitators, to love our enemies, and that is not an easy thing to do. But because we are to be like Him, we have to love our enemies and do good to them. God is kind to everybody because He created everybody with love. He wants us to love one another to prove that we are His sons.

2 Thessalonians 1:11 "Wherefore also we pray always for you, that our God would count you worthy of this calling, and fulfil all the good pleasure of his goodness, and the work of faith with power." "For the fruit of the Spirit is in all goodness and righteousness and truth" (Ephesians 5:9).

One of the key qualities a nonbeliever will pick up on in a solid Christian is this quality of goodness. People with this quality are good down to their very cores of their personalities. This can be easily seen and felt when we one get around people with this quality.

Truly good people cannot use others for their gain. They cannot manipulate other. Many people draw near them because they feel happy and secure when they are with them.

Jesus Christ was kind to everybody and He died for everybody. He did die for specific people. Because of the love He had to everybody, He shows goodness and kindness to all. Even today His kindness and goodness are still applying. He shows His kindness by calling those who are weary and burdened. Matthew 11:28-30 "Come to me, all you who are weary and burdened, and I will give you rest. Take my yoke upon you and learn from me, for I am gentle and humble in heart, and you will find rest for your souls. For my yoke is easy and my burden is light."

If somebody is not kind and good, he cannot help those with heavy loads to carry or cannot carry such loads himself. To carry somebody's load means you help him with whatever is troubling him. Some of the troubles will want us to be gentle with love. We must pray God to help us to resemble Him well on this earth.

Let us pray: "Dear heavenly Father, we thank You for carrying our loads. We ask you to help us to carry the loads of others as you said in your Word in Galatians 6:2-3 We have to share each other's burdens, and in this way we obey the law of Christ. If we think we are too important to help someone, we are only fooling ourselves. We are not that important." We know My Lord that we are unimportant. Please help us to do everything that is important to you. We ask this in Jesus' Name; Amen.

CHAPTER SEVEN

FAITHFULNESS: (Latin *fides*)

Faithfulness is committing us to something, for instance God. Being faithful means not wandering form the truth. It is not easy to be faithful, it takes trust in God.

Christians are called to be faithful by being obedient to God and His Word. Matthew 22:37 "Jesus replied: 'Love the Lord your God with all your heart and with all your soul and with your entire mind.'" If we are really faithful to our God we will definitely love Him with all our hearts, our souls and our minds. We can only do this by applying Proverbs 3:3-4 "Let love and faithfulness never leave you; bind them around your neck, write them on the tablet of your heart. Then you will get favour and a good name in the sight of God and man." If something is around your neck or in your heart, you will always live with it. This is what is needed, i.e. not to allow love and faithfulness to leave us.

Isaiah 11:5 "Righteousness will be his belt and faithfulness the sash around his waist." From the above Scripture of Proverbs 3:3-4: "Let love and faithfulness never leave you; bind them around your neck, write them on the tablet of your heart. Then you will get favour and a good name in the sight of God and man." Here the faithfulness must be around our necks and in Isaiah 11:5 – faithfulness must be the sash around the waist of the branch of Jesse. This means we are to wear faithfulness all over us. It starts with the neck now it goes down to the waist.

Christians must develop a good relationship with God and foster it through prayer, meditation, Bible study, and servant hood. Romans 12:1-2 "Therefore, I urge you, brothers, in view of God's mercy, to offer your bodies as living sacrifices, holy and pleasing to God – this is your spiritual act of worship. Do not confirm any longer to the pattern of this world, but be transformed by the renewing of your mind. Then you will be able to test and approve what God's will is – His good, pleasing and perfect will." God wants us to be transformed, to offer our bodies as living sacrifices. That can happen only if we are faithful to Him. The prayer of Jesus was that we be protected against the evil one (John 17:15).

According to the book *Romans* above, God wants our minds to be renewed with God's Words, our spirit renewed with devotion, and our love for God renewed by taking to Him and by holding on to the first love we experienced when we first met Him.

As Christians we must have the following marks of faithfulness:

- We must do the follow-ups on whatever we have to do.
- We must deliver goods – whether messages or meals to our fellow brothers or where necessary.
- Whether at work, meetings or where are needed to be, we must show up early.
- We must honour commitments and appointments – this shows faithfulness and we must not just cancel for convenience sake. Always communicate or update brothers with the changes
- We must carry our instructions and transact business with respect.
- We must always do the official duties in the church but must not neglect worship. That is offering our bodies as living sacrifices (Romans 12:1-2)
- We must be devoted to the duties of God and must seek the Father's will.

How can we exhibit these marks of faithfulness?

- We must call upon God in prayer and ask Him to help. Psalm 138:3 "When I called, You answered me, you made me bold and stout-hearted."
- We must be honest. Luke 16:10 "Whoever can be trusted with very little can also be trusted with much, and whoever is dishonest with very little will also be dishonest with much."
- We must rely on God's strength. Philippians 4:3 "I can do everything through Him who gives me strength."

- We must fight self-indulgence. 1 Corinthians 9:27 "No, I beat my body and make it my slave so that after I have preached to others, I myself will not be disqualified for the prize."
- Eliminate laziness and idleness. Proverbs 31:27 "She watches over the affairs of her household and does not eat the bred of idleness."
- We must be faithful in all things. Matthew 25:23 "His master replied, 'Well done, good and faithful servant! You have been faithful with a few things; I will put you in charge of many things. Come and share your master's happiness!'"

We must allow God's Spirit to move into all areas of our life so that faithfulness becomes a way of life for us as mentioned earlier in this chapter that we must wear faithfulness in our necks and on our waists. We must meditate the following verses so that people around us will be able to see the love of God through our faithful living: Isaiah 25:1 "O Lord, though art my God; I will exalt thee, I will praise thy name; for thou hast done wonderful things; thy counsels of old are faithfulness and truth." Ephesians 3:16-17 "I pray that our God will grant you according to His glorious riches to be strengthened with power through his Spirit in your inner being, so that Christ may dwell in your hearts through faith."

We must have faith in our Lord so that our faithfulness can be committed to Him. We cannot commit ourselves to God if we do not trust. We must put our trust in God because he is also faithful. He promised not to leave us nor forsake us. He is our Omnipresent God because He is always present in all situations.

Let us pray: "Dear heavenly Father, we praise You because You are faithful to us. We will sing you songs of praise at all times, because You are with us at all times. You protect, provide, heal and prosper us. We ask You to help us to be faithful to You and to others because of the faithfulness you showed to us. We ask this in the faithful name of our Lord Jesus Christ; Amen."

CHAPTER EIGHT

TEMPERANCE (SELF CONTROL): (Latin: *continentia*)

The Greek word for self-control is *enkrateia.* Self-control goes with gentleness.
1 Corinthians 7:5 "Do not deprive each other except by mutual consent and for a time, so that you may devote yourselves to prayer. Then come together again so that Satan will not tempt you because of your lack of self-control." Self-control is necessary because we are at war with our own sinful desires. We must always pray to God to control us. God knows us inside and outside. He knows our plans even before we can act on them. We need the protection of our God because bad plans are from the Devil.

Christians must be happy because Jesus Christ promised us the Holy Spirit. John 14:26 "But the Counsellor, the Holy Spirit, whom the Father will send in my name, will teach you all things and will remind you of everything I have said to you." It is important that we not only listen to Holy Spirit but also act upon what He is revealing to us what is offensive and against God.

We must be like our God in being slow to anger. Psalm 86:15 "But you, O Lord, are a compassionate and gracious God, slow to anger, and abounding in love and faithfulness." In most cases, people provoke God with all bad actions, but it takes God a long time to anger. We should strive to be more like God. The Bible teaches us to bless our enemies and pray for them and love them. Mostly our enemies are those who made us angry, but the Scripture advise us to pray for them. Luke 6:28 "Bless those who curse you, pray for those who mistreat you." People who mistreat us always make us angry.

Luke 22:40 "Pray that you will not fall into temptation." Once we fell into temptation, it means we lack self-control. God is advising us in Ephesians 4:26-27 "In your anger do not sin. Do not let the sun go down while you are still angry, and do not give the devil a foothold. God will not fail us not forsake us. Self-control is the key; we must strive to grow in our faith and Godliness. Sound judgment is the beginning of self-control, and sound judgment must be based on the knowledge of God's Word and His standard for our bodies, thoughts and emotions. Sound judgment enables us to make and accurately estimate all our needs in the area of self-control.

2 Peter 4:2 "But also for this very reason, giving all diligence, add to your faith virtue, to virtue knowledge, to knowledge self-control, to self-control perseverance, to perseverance godliness, to godliness brotherly kindness and to brotherly kindness love."

It is important for Christians to call upon the Spirit of God to help us in our time of need, realizing that we cannot accomplish this without His help and leadership. We must always choose what is right in the eyes of our Lord.

Self-control is the last on the list of the fruit of the spirit. It simply means that Christians must have all other fruits first and it is then that they can control themselves. Love is the first one on the list. This must be like that because the first love was shown by God when He created heavens and earth and everything including us in His image.

God did all these with joy. If this did not make Him happy He could have not created us and everything on earth. During the time of creation He had peace and He was patient because He did not just in one day made everything even if He could. He want to make sure that everything is done in a gentle manner with kindness and goodness. That is why every time He finished He would say it if good – it is perfect. Because of His faithfulness, He did not want to destroy his creation and He promised the serpent that 14 Then the Lord God said to the serpent that: "Because you have done this, you are cursed more than all animals, domestic and wild. You will crawl on your belly; grovelling in the dust as long as you live.15 And I will cause hostility between you and the woman, and between your offspring and her offspring. He will strike your head, and you will strike his heel" (Genesis 3:14-15).

These fruits of the spirit originated from our Father and that is why He desires that we have them so that He can use the gifts of the spirit well in us. 1 Corinthians 12:8-11 "For to one is given the word of wisdom through the Spirit, to another the word of knowledge through the same Spirit, to another faith by the same Spirit, to another gifts of healings by the same Spirit, to another the working of miracles, to another prophecy, to another discerning of spirits, to another different kinds of tongues, to another the interpretation of tongues. But one and the same Spirit works all these things, distributing to each one individually as He wills."

CONCLUSION

God has given each believer a combination of opportunities and gifts that are perfectly suited to his or her situation in life. Every Christian is really a minister with a unique contribution to make to the body of Christ. The central thrust of our ministry depends on the spiritual gifts we have received. The Spiritual gifts we received will minister well with Spiritual fruit. Many believers have received more than one spiritual gift. According to 1 Peter 4:10-11; our spiritual gifts are ultimately designed to glorify God. As we use our spiritual gifts in conjunction with the power and fruit (especially love) of the Holy Spirit and in the name of the Lordship of Jesus Christ, the Father receives the glory.

If we want to enjoy the fruit and minister and glorify God by the gifts of the Spirit; we must ask ourselves the following questions:

- Have I received Christ as my Savoir? Unlike natural talents, spiritual gifts are bestowed only on Christians.

- Am I walking in fellowship with the Lord? To be effective, spiritual gifts must be manifested in the context of the fruit of the Holy Spirit. This fruit is impeded by unconfessed sin and a failure to abide in Christ. "Remain in me, and I in you. Just as the branch in unable to produce fruit by itself unless it remains on the vine, so neither can you unless you remain in ME" (John 15:4).

- Do I really want to develop my gift(s)? A prerequisite to knowing your gifts is a willingness to go through the effort to be involved in discovering and developing them.

We must ask God to show us our gifts. God desires us to discover and implement the gifts He has given us and this is a request we can make with confidence and expectation. "Do not worry about anything, but within everything through prayer and petition with thanksgiving, let your requests be made known to God. And the

50

peace of God, which surpassed every thought, will guard your hearts and your minds in Christ Jesus." (Philippians 4:6-7).

We must expose ourselves to biblical teaching on spiritual gifts by studying Romans 12, 1 Corinthians 12-12 and Ephesians 4. Books on Spiritual gifts could be helpful. We must associate with people who clearly know their spiritual gifts and ask them how they discovered them.

God is committed to us to have joy not to be miserable. We must take delight in God because He always answers our prayers. Just as we discover our natural talents by trying our hand at numerous things, in the same manner we can discover our spiritual gifts by experimenting with several of the available gifts. If we do not try, we will never know and be perfect. Availability and willingness to learn our weaknesses as well as strength is required. God work with the availability, not the qualification. Until we are able, God will use us, and a lot of practice is needed.

As we use our gifts in the power of the Spirit, God will confirm and establish us in our ministry, and there will be positive feedback from those to whom we ministered, and our Lord will be glorified.

Let us pray: "Dear heavenly Father, we pray in the wonder-working Name of our Lord Jesus Christ that we need this fruit of the spirit, so that we can serve you well on this earth. We know that we cannot have these fruit if You are not in our lives. We ask You right now in Jesus Name to enter in our hearts and control our lives, so that we can be able to do your will at all times. Holy Spirit, we are asking You as our Teacher, Helper, Advocate and Counsellor to be with us at all times so that we resemble our Lord well. We are asking this in the powerful name of our Lord Jesus Christ; Amen."

BIBLICAL REFERENCES

1. Genesis 3:14-15
2. Leviticus 19:18 NIV
3. Numbers 6:26, 22:21-34
4. Deuteronomy 4:20, 16:15
5. Joshua 1:9
6. 2 Samuel 11:1-27
7. 2 Chronicles 16:8
8. Nehemiah 8:10
9. Esther 9:22
10. Job 1:21, 42:10
11. Psalm 34:14, 37:3, 51:12, 86:15, 94: 11-13, 138:3
12. Proverbs 3:3-4, 3:5, 11:28, 28:26, 31:27
13. Isaiah 9:6, 11:5, 25:1, 35:10
14. Jeremiah 3:22, 29:11
15. Lamentations 3:22-23
16. Matthew 5:44-45, 6:25-35, 11:28-30, 22:37, 25:23, 25:31-46
17. Mark 1:40-41
18. Luke 6:28, 6:35, 16:10, 22:40, 23:23
19. John 3:7 NIV, 3:16-17, 14:6, 14:26, 14:27, 15:11, 15:13, 15:4 & 19, 16:3, 17:15
20. Acts 14:17
21. Romans 2:4, 5:1-2, 5:1, 13, 5:18-19, 8:28, 8:31, 8:38-39, 12:1-2, 15:13
22. 1 Corinthian 7:5, 9:27, 13:4-8 &10,
23. 2 Corinthians 4:18, 5:6-7, 5:18-19, 21, 12:9
24. Galatians 5:22-23 (New King James Version)
25. Galatians 5:22-23 (New International Reader's Version)
26. Galatians 5:1,13, 24-25
27. Galatians 6:1,2-3
28. Ephesians 3:16-17, 4:2, 4:26-27, 5:9
29. Philippians 4:3, 4:4, 4:6-7, 4:13, 4:19
30. Colossians 3:12
31. 1 Thessalonians 5:14, 5:16
32. 2 Thessalonians 1:11, 5:18
33. 1 Timothy 1:16
34. 2 Timothy 2:24-26, 4:2

35. Hebrews 12:2   , 12:6
36. James 1:2-4,5:10-11
37. James 5:7-8
38. 1 Peter 3:15-16, 4:10-11, 5:7
39. 2 Peter 1:5-9, 3:9,3:15, 4:2,
40. 1 John 1:9, 2:15-17, 4:4, 4:7, 4:9-10, 4:16
41. Revelation 3:19

John Ritenbaugh

www.ingramcontent.com/pod-product-compliance
Lightning Source LLC
Chambersburg PA
CBHW060623030426
42337CB00018B/3164